DTN YP

P9-DVU-724

DISCARDED

goal.

9.   When the ball goes out of bounds it shall be thrown into the field, and played by the person first touching it.   In case of a dispute the umpire shall throw it straight into the field. The thrower in is allowed five seconds, if he holds it longer it shall go to the opponent.   If any side presists in delaying the game, the umpire shall call a foul on them.

10. The umpire shall be judge of the men, and shall note the fouls, and notify the referee when three consecutive fouls have been made.   He shall have power to disqualify men according to Rule 5.

11.   The referee shall be judge of the ball and shall decide when the ball is in play, in bounds, and to which side it belongs, and shall keep the time.   He shall decide when a goal has been made, and keep account of the goals with any other duties that are usually performed by a referee.

12.   The time shall be two fifteen minutes halves, with five minutes rest between.

13.   The side making the most goals in that time shall be declared the winners.   In case of a draw the game may, by agreement of the captains, be continued until another goal is made.

First draft of Basket Ball rules.
Hung in the gym that the boys might
learn the rules — Dec, 1891   James Naismith
6-28-31.

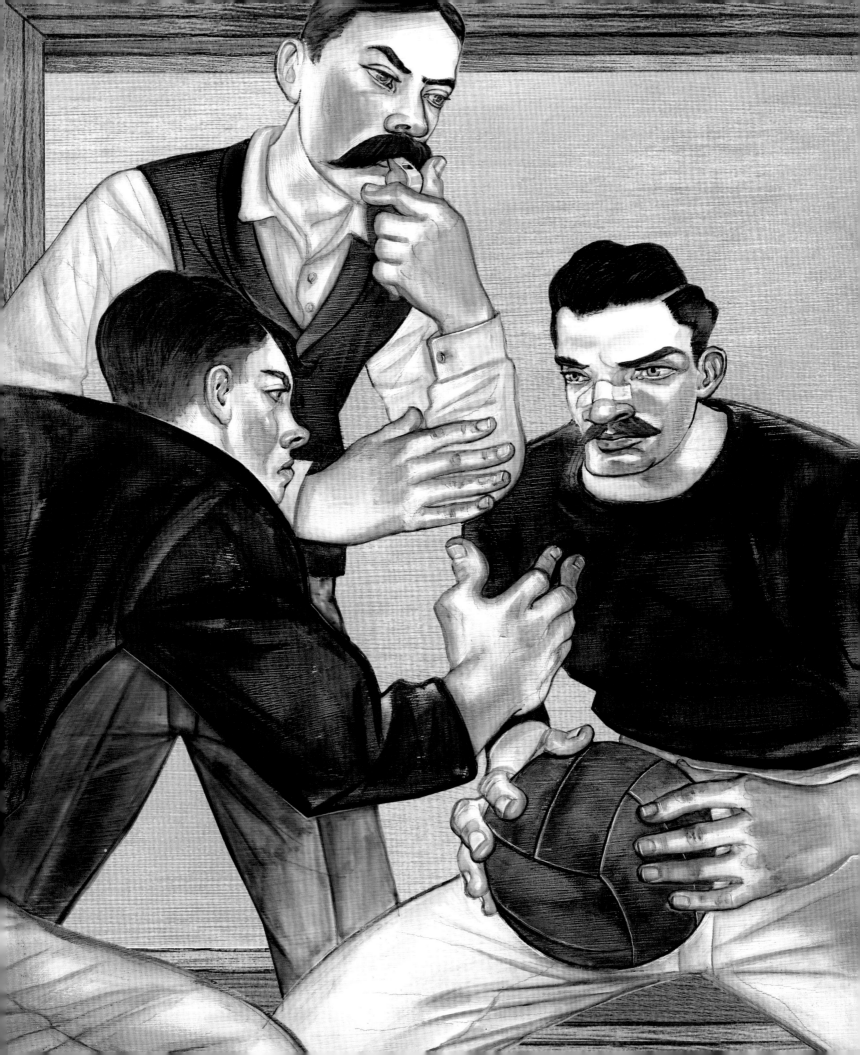

HOOP GENIUS

HOW A DESPERATE TEACHER AND A ROWDY GYM CLASS

INVENTED BASKETBALL

JOHN COY

illustrations by
JOE MORSE

CAROLRHODA BOOKS • MINNEAPOLIS

In December of 1891, James Naismith, a young teacher, took over a rowdy gym class that had already forced two teachers to quit.

He didn't want to, but
nobody else would teach
that class.

...indoor football.

He needed something
much less rough.

The next day, Naismith
suggested indoor soccer.

He called a halt.

In desperation, he turned to his favorite sport, lacrosse.

Nothing was working with this group.

Naismith felt like giving up but couldn't. The boys in the class reminded him of how he'd been at their age—energetic, impatient, and eager for something exciting.

He needed a totally new game where, to avoid tackling, no running with the ball was allowed. He remembered playing Duck on a Rock as a boy. In that game, you knocked an opponent's fist-sized stone off a larger rock by throwing your own.

If you missed, you had to retrieve your stone before you were tagged, so accuracy was more valuable than force.

He snapped his fingers and said, "I've got it." How about a game with a goal off the ground that required an arcing throw?

That night he stayed up late thinking about the new game.

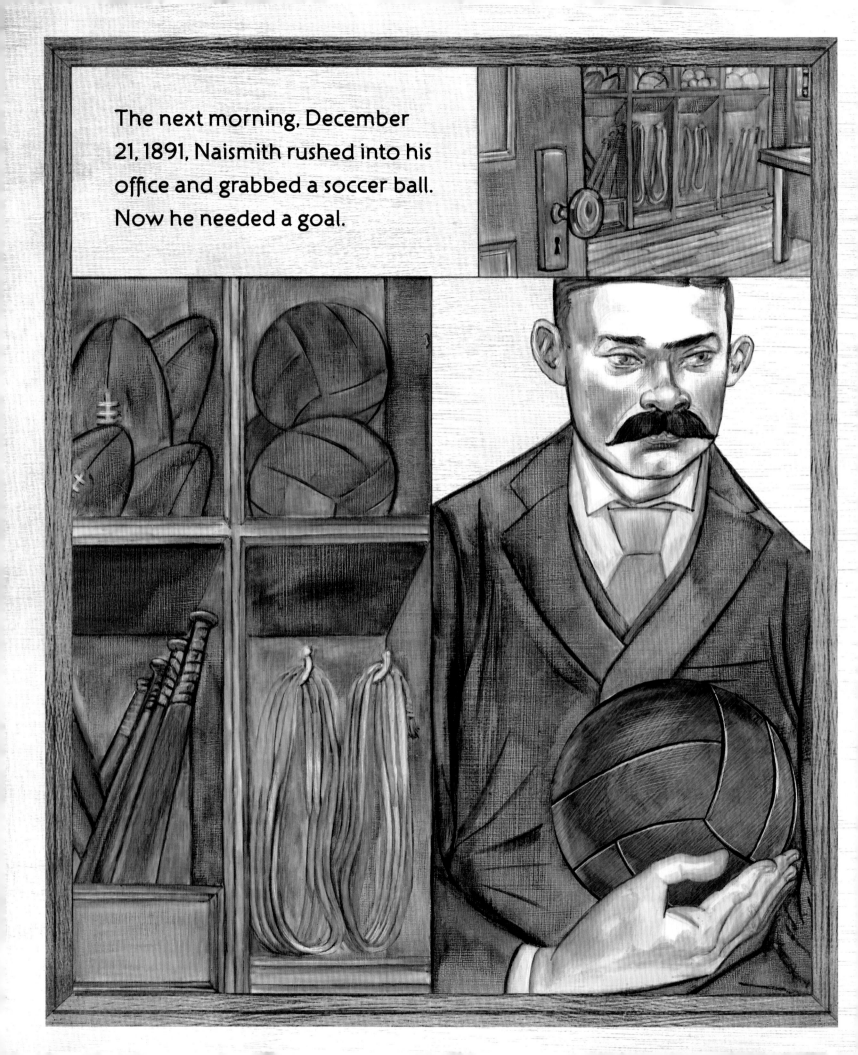

The next morning, December 21, 1891, Naismith rushed into his office and grabbed a soccer ball. Now he needed a goal.

He asked Pop Stebbins, the building superintendent, for a couple of square boxes. He didn't have them, but he had something else—two old peach baskets.

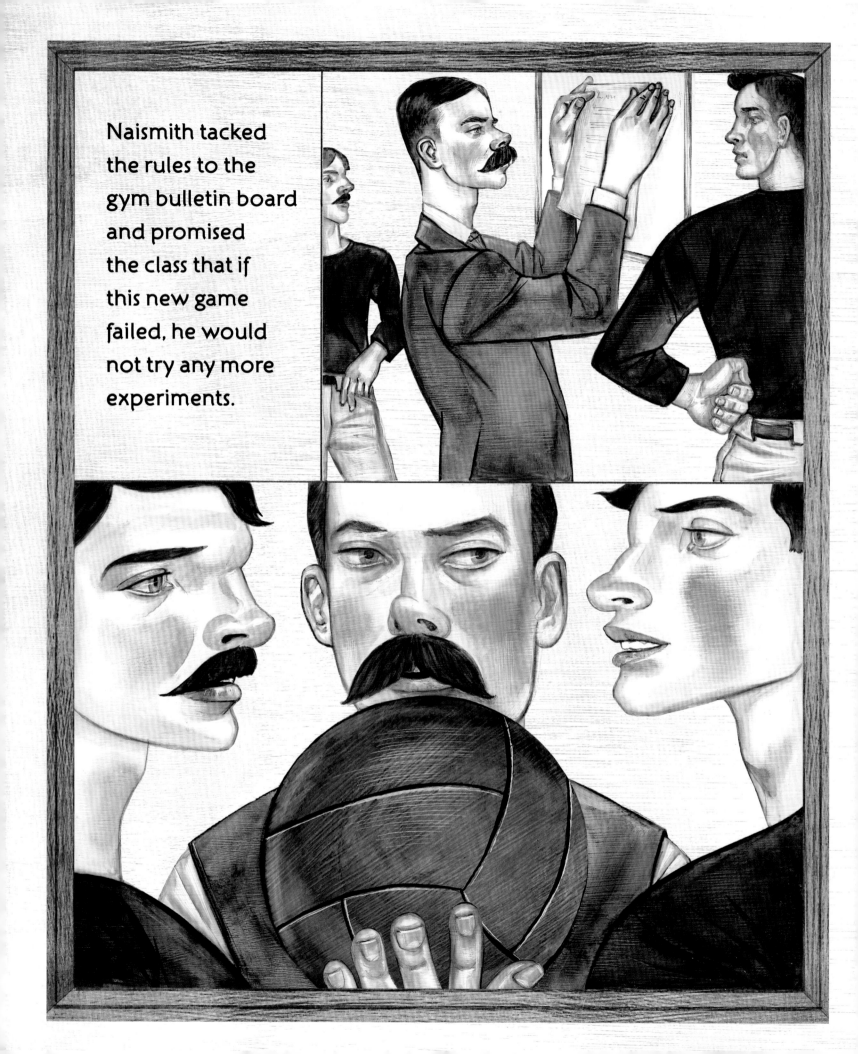

Naismith tacked the rules to the gym bulletin board and promised the class that if this new game failed, he would not try any more experiments.

Captains chose teams of nine members, and Naismith selected two center men. He tossed the ball up between them, and they jumped for it to start the new game.

Because the men had never played before, Naismith called many fouls for holding, pushing, and tripping. After two fouls, the player had to sit on the sideline until the next goal occurred.

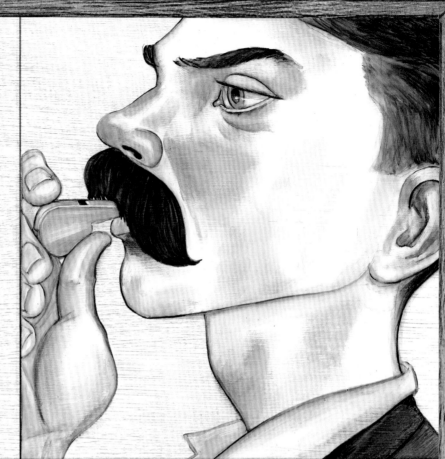

William Chase launched a shot from twenty-five feet …

...that went in for the first and only basket of the game.

When Naismith blew the whistle to end the game, nobody wanted to leave.

The next day, the students lined up eagerly for the game.

They played hard but avoided fouling because they wanted to stay on the court.

When students went home for Christmas vacation, they taught the new game to their friends. Soon people in cities, small towns, and on farms were playing basketball.

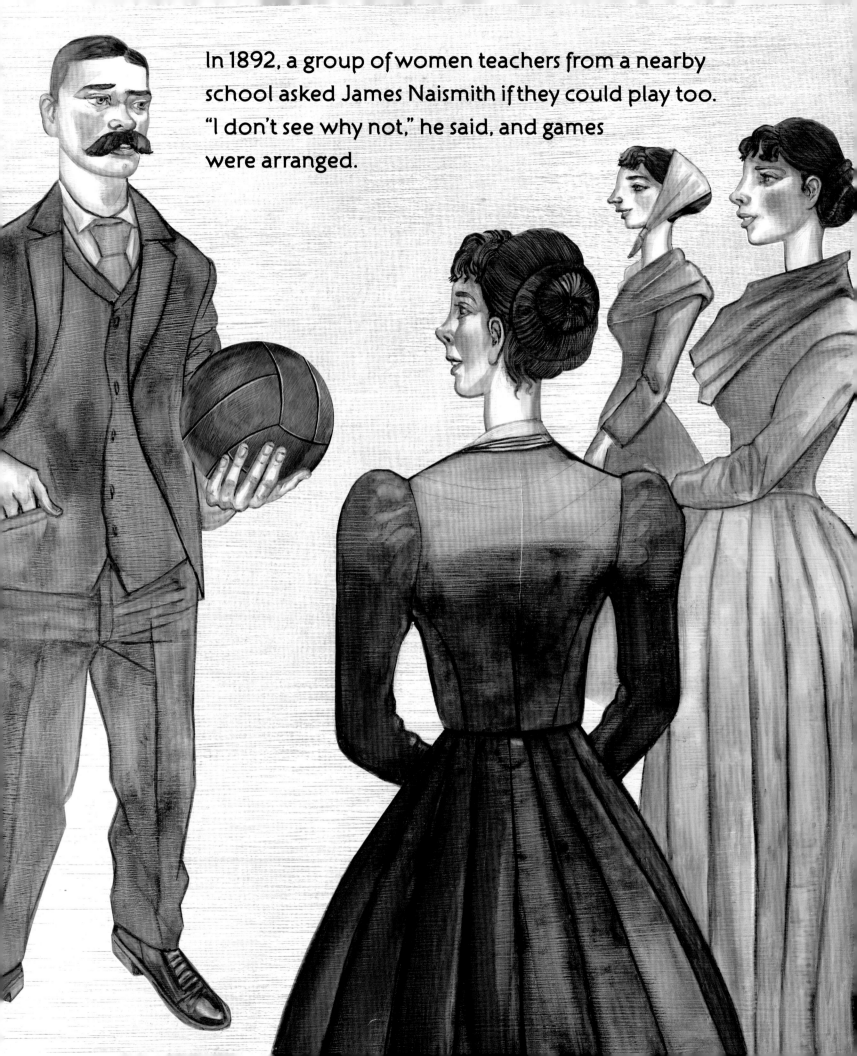

In 1892, a group of women teachers from a nearby school asked James Naismith if they could play too. "I don't see why not," he said, and games were arranged.

In one of them, Naismith, as referee, was shocked when he called a foul and one of the women protested as strongly as any man. But he remembered that game clearly. One of the women, Maude Sherman, later became his wife.

By 1936, basketball was so popular around the world that it became an Olympic sport. James Naismith attended the opening ceremonies, and when each nation dipped its flag to honor him, tears of happiness came to his eyes.

And today, millions of people around the world play the game that was invented by James Naismith and that rowdy class. Do you?

For the game. —J.C.

For Lorraine, my partner in all things. —J.M.

Text copyright © 2013 by John Coy
Illustrations copyright © 2013 by Joe Morse

All rights reserved. International copyright secured. No part of this book may be reproduced, stored in a retrieval system, or transmitted in any form or by any means—electronic, mechanical, photocopying, recording, or otherwise—without the prior written permission of Lerner Publishing Group, Inc., except for the inclusion of brief quotations in an acknowledged review.

Carolrhoda Books
A division of Lerner Publishing Group, Inc.
241 First Avenue North
Minneapolis, MN 55401 U.S.A.

Website address: www.lernerbooks.com

Additional images in this book are used with the permission of: AP Photo/Bebeto Matthews (Photographs of Dr. James Naismith's Original 13 Rules of Basket Ball. The documents are now kept at the University of Kansas in Lawrence.); © Hulton Archive/Getty Images (Naismith with his first basketball team).

Main body text set in Atelier Sans ITC Std Bold 17/25.
Typeface provided by International Typeface Corp.

Library of Congress Cataloging-in-Publication Data

Coy, John.
    Hoop genius : how a desperate teacher and a rowdy gym class invented basketball / by John Coy ; illustrated by Joe Morse.
      p.   cm.
    ISBN: 978-0-7613-6617-1 (lib. bdg. : alk. paper)
    1. Basketball—United States—History—Juvenile literature. 2. Naismith, James, 1861–1939—Juvenile literature. I. Morse, Joe, 1960- ill. II. Title.
    GV885.1.C68 2013
    796.323'2—dc23   2011021235

Manufactured in the United States of America
1 – PC – 12/31/12

Author's Note

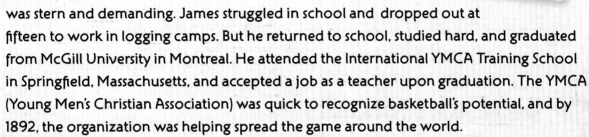

James Naismith (1861–1939) suffered the loss of
both his parents to typhoid fever by the time he
was nine, and he was raised by his Uncle Peter who
was stern and demanding. James struggled in school and dropped out at
fifteen to work in logging camps. But he returned to school, studied hard, and graduated
from McGill University in Montreal. He attended the International YMCA Training School
in Springfield, Massachusetts, and accepted a job as a teacher upon graduation. The YMCA
(Young Men's Christian Association) was quick to recognize basketball's potential, and by
1892, the organization was helping spread the game around the world.

• • •

A number of people shared valuable information with me about James Naismith and
the creation of basketball including John Gossett, who showed me the original stone
from Duck on a Rock and connected me with John Dunn, who led a memorable tour
of Naismith sites around Almonte, Ontario. The staff at the Naismith Memorial Basketball
Hall of Fame in Springfield, Massachusetts, provided important documents, as did Jeffrey
Monseau, archivist at Springfield College, and Ryan Bean at the YMCA Archives at the
University of Minnesota. Thank you to them and, above all, to Dr. Naismith and that rowdy
class for this great game.

Selected Bibliography

Naismith, James. *Basketball, Its Origin and Development.* New York: Association Press, 1941.

Naismith, James. "How Basketball Started and Why It Grew." *Journal of Physical Education,* November 1932.

Naismith, James. *Rules for Basketball.* Springfield, MA: Triangle Publishing Company, 1892.

Rains, Rob. *James Naismith: The Man Who Invented Basketball.* With Hellen Carpenter. Philadelphia: Temple University Press, 2009.

Webb, Bernice Larson. *The Basketball Man: James Naismith.* Lawerence: University Press of Kansas, 1973.

0000121838858

Basket Ball

The ball to be an ordinary Association foot ball.

1. The ball may be thrown in any direction with one or both hands.

2. The ball may be batted in any direction with one or both hands (never with the fist).

3. A player cannot run with the ball, the player must throw it from the spot on which he catches it, allowance to be made for a man who catches the ball when running at a good speed.

4. The ball must ~~be held in or between the hands,~~ the arms or body must not be used for holding it.

5. No shouldering, holding, pushing, tripping or striking, in any way the person of an opponent shall be allowed. The first infringement of this rule by any person shall count as a foul, the second shall disqualify him until the next goal is made, or if there was evident intent to injure the person, for the whole of the game , no substitute allowed.

6. A foul is striking at the ball with the fist, violation of rules 3 and 4, and such as described in rule 5.

7. If ~~either~~ side ~~makes three consecutive~~ fouls it shall count a goal for the opponents (consecutive means without the opponents in the meantime making a foul).

8. A goal shall be made when the ball is thrown or batted from the grounds into the basket and stays there, providing those defending the goal do not touch or disturbe the goal. If the ball rests on the edge and the opponent moves the basket it shall count as a